# What If There Is Nothing Wrong With You?

## A Practice in Reinterpretation

Susan Munich Henkels, MSW

This book is dedicated to my parents, for without them none of this would have been possible ... in more ways than one. To my Aunt Norma Jean and Aunt Vivian who assured me there was nothing wrong with me in the first place!

*What If There Is Nothing
Wrong With You*
— a Book and a Practice —

- Dissolve and dismantle your belief
  that something is wrong with you and
  replace that belief with *it is what it is*
  ... exactly that, nothing more, nothing
  less.

- Redefine your personal path to a new
  interpretation of right and wrong.

- Discover the satisfaction of adopting
  this new perspective, and how to best
  use it every day for a more productive
  and fulfilling life.

# Prologue

There was a very poor old man who lived in a small village and even kings were jealous of him because he had a beautiful white horse. They had offered fabulous prices for the horse, and the man would continue to say, "This horse is not a horse to me, he is a person. How could I sell a person, a friend?" The man was very poor but he would never sell his horse.

One morning, he discovered that the horse was not in the stable. The whole village gathered and said, "You foolish old man! We knew that someday that horse would be stolen. It surely would have been better to sell it. What a misfortune!"

The old man replied, "Don't say that. Simply say what

IS - that the horse is not in the stable. That is the fact. Everything else is a judgment. Whether it is a misfortune or a blessing, I don't know, because this is just a fragment of the story."

People laughed at the old man as they had always known that he was a little crazy. But after fifteen days, suddenly one night the horse returned. Not only had he not been stolen but he brought back a dozen wild horses with him.

Again the people of the village gathered around and said, "Old man, you were right. This was not a misfortune, as it has indeed proved to be a blessing."

The old man said, "Don't say that. Just say what IS - the horse is back with a dozen other horses. Who knows whether it is a blessing or not? It is only a fragment."

This time the people did not say much but inside they knew that he was wrong, especially as they were watching his only son begin to train the wild horses. How could this not be a blessing?

Just a week later, his son fell from one of the horses

and broke both of his legs. The people gathered and again they judged. "You have proven to be right. It was indeed a misfortune. Your only son has lost the use of his legs and was your only support in your old age. Now you are poorer than ever."

The old man said, "You are obsessed with judgment. Don't say what you are saying. Say only what IS - that my son has broken his legs. Nobody knows whether this is a misfortune or a blessing. Life comes in fragments and more is never given to you."

It happened that after a few weeks the country went to war, and all the young men of the town were forcibly taken for the military. Only the old man's son was left because he was crippled. The whole town was crying and weeping because it was a losing battle and they knew most of the young people would never come back.

They came to the old man and said, "You were right, old man, this has proved a blessing. Maybe your son is crippled, but he is still with you. Our sons are gone forever."

The old man said, "You go on and on judging. Nobody knows! Only say that your sons have been forced to enter the army and my son has not been forced. With fragments you will be obsessed with small things and jump to conclusions. Once you judge, you have stopped growing."

Author Unknown, permission to reprint being sought

*Anything that forces people to have to think is not an easy sell, but when we want to shake things up and instigate change, it may be necessary to break free of familiar thought patterns and easy assumptions. We have to veer off the beaten neural path. We do this in large part by questioning.*

~Warren Berger, *A More Beautiful Question*~

# 1

*The highest form of human intelligence
is to observe yourself without judgement.*
~ Krishnamurti

The spirit of the book and practice *What If There
Is Nothing Wrong With You* is perfectly described in
the quote by Warren Berger that you read on the previous
page, where he asserts that questioning causes us to veer
from our familiar patterns and assumptions. I would add
that we also do this by reinterpreting long held concepts,
such as our definitions of right and wrong.

In my career as a psychotherapist, I've come to think

of life as a twenty foot wall and when we're born we're given a sixteen foot ladder. Much of our climb up the ladder of life is accomplished using decisions we made in the first five years of our lives, with behaviors we adopted in order to survive circumstances we didn't have the skills to understand. And yet, as an adult when we finally reach what seems like the top rung of the ladder, we look around and think: oh no!

Regardless of how well we believe we know ourselves, hopefully at this point on the ladder we realize the early decisions that got us this far will NOT get us over the wall. Staring up at the final four feet, it dawns on us that we have actually outlived the usefulness of our early story and we won't make it much further by holding on to our early interpretation of this story.

I believe that around four or five we make some brilliant intuitive decisions about what we need to do in order to navigate the landmines of our earliest experiences. To intuitively adopt these survival techniques is a brilliant strategy for a child to make, a child without the benefit of an adequate vocabulary and without the skills to ask direct questions. Imagine the young mind making these decisions while already overwhelmed with input from the surrounding circumstances.

The good news is the early stories we created successfully supported us to where we are now. There's nothing wrong with that. But you may not make it up over those last four feet of wall with old decisions that are more about surviving rather than thriving. Possibly a whole new way of thinking is needed to finally get over that wall, to where the juice and joy of life that we have been longing for has been waiting our discovery. Yes, now is time for us to give up living as if something is wrong with us. Once a new perspective is reached, we can get on with living our fullest and most creative lives.

As a therapist, I've been listening to what's wrong with people for over forty-five years. I'm forever grateful for the day when, as I listened to a client's list of all her judgments and criticisms of herself, I thought to myself: what if there is actually nothing wrong with her? What if answering that question could clear the way for her to do anything she wanted to do, without all the self-incriminating limits she was so sure she was right about?

Now I ask you: what if there IS nothing wrong with you? Think about this question for a moment. For now, I'm not saying there ISN'T, simply asking what if there isn't? How could that realization change your relationship with yourself? How could it change your relationship with others? Would you have more confidence and courage to do something you are secretly passionate about? I'm into my seventies and am finally learning to play the banjo which has been on my bucket list for years! Perhaps, if you believed there was nothing wrong with you, you would be more open to learning a new language, being the artist you always wished you could be, starting a garden, going back to school, doing volunteer work, or getting involved politically.

Until I was introduced to the parable of the very poor old man you read about in the prologue, I would get annoyed when I heard the current catch phrase *it is what it is*. This phrase seemed like the new mantra for putting up with a large overload of unwanted reality, a popular throw away response that had little meaning other than leaving people empty and without the possibility of solving anything or changing anything for themselves. Just complete resignation. This phrase provides an effective strategy because you can't argue with it. It stops any constructive communication in its tracks. On the converse there are situations where using it is perfectly justified, such as the weather, game scores, fake news from either side, or any situation that's out of your control. But I am not talking about these.

But, what if *what is*, really is simply *what it is*? A state of being with no right, no wrong, no judgment, or no criticism; a life without the stories we use as excuses to justify, defend, to make ourselves right and others wrong.

Although I started out writing this book for you, the reader, from a life-threatening personal experience

I can attest to the liberating reward of this practice. Five years ago I was diagnosed with a condition that required I undergo open heart surgery. The panic around this was overwhelming and I wasn't certain that holding fast to the belief that there was nothing wrong with me was going to cut it. I'll talk more about this in a following chapter but suffice it to say for now, my book subject got tested to the maximum.

I could not make up the coming together of the unanticipated circumstances and the new perspective I'd developed as the basis of this practice. It both renewed my life and also reaffirmed my belief in letting *what is be what is.*

When considering this new perspective, we must recognize that our commitment to the right or wrong judgments that have supported us for so long, might make a change of perspective seem impossible or unattainable. But as you work deeper into this practice, you will recognize that although the mind becomes deeply ingrained in interpretations of right and wrong, a change of mind is indeed possible. Now the question becomes how to release the set of early beliefs that have limited how we have experienced our lives. The answer I offer is with desire and with practice we can shrink these limitations. Not to mention the enticement of what might be waiting over your twenty foot wall. But first a decision must be made as to what to do with the many interpretations and judgments that have supported your survival and defined how you have described yourself for a very long time.

And what if there really is nothing wrong with you? What a concept. Recently, when I shared the theme of this book with a friend, her response was: "Well now, we wouldn't be very interesting, would we?" Pondering her answer, I began thinking about how much time and energy we spend talking about all that's wrong with ourselves and with the world. Often that's the only way we relate to each other.

It's true that very early in our lives most of us started creating a list of what we thought was wrong with us. Many of the messages we accumulated were sent to us from somebody else, but in our innocence we believed them to be true. We then made adult decisions based on our childhood interpretations.

Wouldn't it be nice if we could stop fighting ourselves, stop being our own worst enemy and move on with our lives without the debilitating drag of believing that we have something to fix all the time? What I'm suggesting is a practice of dissolving judgment, blame and criticism of yourself and others, then replacing those responses with the attitude that the circumstance are what they are, the situation *is what it is*, and the person is simply who they are, doing the best they can at the time.

With that goal in mind, the purpose of this book: *What if There's Nothing Wrong With You?* becomes an inquiry worth having.

# 2

*The moment we hesitate to tell the truth
that is in us, and are silent when we
should speak, the divine floods of light
and life no longer flow into our souls.*

~Elizabeth Cady Stanton

We begin this journey by going within. The first step is discovering and identifying our primary seed stories, the life-shaping and perspective-forming events that occurred in our youth and continue to impact us through adulthood.

Yes, each and every one of us has at least one seed story.

Most of us have a sense of the events that happened in our home or family when we were a child. Although it is likely we can identify many of the events, there are undoubtedly many that we don't remember. This does not lessen their impact.

My story began when tragedy struck our family. I was four and my brother Dick, seven, when life as we'd known it changed overnight. My father, a charismatic, dominating and self-centered man, suffered a cerebral vascular aneurysm at age forty-two. The aneurysm left his entire right side paralyzed. He lost all ability to speak coherently. Severe damage to his brain left him with the inevitable psychological trauma.

Until the cascading set of circumstances that changed our lives forever, I was a happy and creative, self-expressed little girl, always asking a million questions. But the shock of this abrupt, unexplained and unprocessed event closed me down completely. There was nobody present who had the answers or the time to help sort it out for me. Severe punishments for my questioning taught me that keeping my mouth shut was a good way to survive. Because I now believed there was something wrong with everything I said and how I said it, I became wary of saying anything at all. It became safer to keep quiet. In fact it became a matter of survival to be silent.

To believe there was nothing wrong with me seemed like a faraway fantasy land and an impossible question to entertain. These beliefs left me to start on my journey to adulthood with the decisions I made at age five about how I should navigate my life. It would take many years for me to question whether there was something wrong with me, or not, as a serious inquiry.

My mother, age twenty-nine at the time, was left to deal with her own terror and frustration. My brother and I lost both parents in one fell swoop. Our father was lost to the effects of the stroke and our mother lost to us by having to attend to his every need. In our mother's frustration at her own helplessness, she would often lash out with harsh, painful slaps to the face when we said the wrong thing or asked the wrong questions. We were confused about what would upset her and withheld asking for help that we needed. Using my voice felt wrong and worse, very scary. Since there were no encouraging parents present, my brother and I turned to each other as the only safe, compassionate space that was available. I have said often that he saved my life as a loving presence and we are both grateful that we were able to serve as witness for each other to the horror that was really happening.

The message I received was to be a lovely child and act like everything was fine, to be a nice little girl even when I didn't feel nice. And definitely to hold inside my fear and anger about what was happening around me. There was no safe place to say anything that would reveal the secret of our miserable family.

After returning from six months of extensive physical and emotional rehabilitation, my father still struggled with relearning to speak. Often his own frustration led to uncontrollable outbursts of loud, angry swearing, and humiliating verbal abuse.

I remember clearly trying to help him by finishing his sentences when he couldn't find the words. Of course, at my tender age there was no way I could understand the paradox of his need to be helped and concurrently his not wanting any help. At the age when I was just beginning to find my own words and to express my own feelings and needs, I was completely confused by the chaotic responses and indiscriminant punishments during his long recovery process. So, just as I was beginning to find my own voice, it disappeared. I made a decision that I wouldn't ask, wouldn't need.

Things got much worse when my father realized he would never return to being the whole man he was before the aneurysm. His unpredictable outbursts of rage would flair without warning and left me unable to guess what might have sparked his disapproval and anger. I might have laughed too loud at the dinner table, complained about what we were eating, wore a red dress that he hated.  For months the only words available to him were GODDAMNSONOFABITCHSHIT.

There's a family story still told about me, when at age six I joined my parents' anniversary celebration.  When nobody was looking, I drained the half-filled champagne glasses, turned several circles in the middle of the room, said "GODDAMNSONOFABITCHSHIT," then passed out cold!  Clearly, I wanted someone to hear that something was not quite right.

As time went on the list of what was wrong with me got longer and longer.  The climate had been perfect for me to begin making up a very imaginative and creative story about myself.

Later came the years of my own therapy, trying to fix all that I thought was broken in me. I read books that I was sure would have the answers and participated in every human potential training I could get myself into. After I earned a master's in social work, I worked with others on what they believed was wrong with them. After all, I could relate to their perspective.  In fact,

I probably started my work as a 'therapist' as early as first grade when on the playground I was already facilitating arguments between my friends. Later when I was asked what I wanted to do when I grew up, I only had to notice what I had already been doing for years. Becoming a therapist seemed an obvious choice. I knew I wanted to create a more conscious roadmap for myself, and also for others to know and feel better about themselves and about their lives.

During my own healing time, I continued to wonder if there were other ways beyond the interpretation of right and wrong. I wondered if any of us really want to let go of things that are so deeply ingrained in our minds. And even more challenging, I questioned what we should do with the interpretations and judgments that defined how we had been describing ourselves and others. Resigning to the mindset of *it is what it is* seemed too simplistic for our complicated lives. But, in spite of the questioning, I was determined to plough on. I did, and so can you.

# Suggested Personal Practices

- Write the story you tell about yourself.
  Begin when you first felt something was
  wrong. Who told you that something
  was wrong with you? Did you have
  an ally in any part of your story?

- Make a list of what you believe is wrong with
  you now, including the physical, spiritual,
  emotional, and physical aspects of yourself.

# 3

*I'm interested in that drive, that rush to judgment that is so prevalent in our society. We all know that pleasurable rush that comes from condemning, and in the short term, it's quite a satisfying thing to do, isn't it?* ~ J.K. Rowling

Let's face it, without an incentive to move out of our comfort zone it's easier to live in a comfortable right or wrong interpretation, the familiar way we have created to define ourselves. I don't believe we hold onto anything for very long that is not providing us with some benefit. Perhaps the mind gets so busy with beating ourselves up with our incessant criticisms and judgments that it actually thinks it's accomplishing something! Satisfying, isn't it?

It's easy to see that if we make ourselves wrong long enough we can justify any number of things, including procrastination, which puts a smokescreen in front of anything we might want to accomplish. Including not taking responsibility for our own talent and power, having a false sense of humility, not speaking up for what is important to us, keeping quiet out of fear of criticism, and so many more. Criticizing ourselves works really well to keep the decision of not doing anything hardwired into place. We end up interpreting these decisions as benefits.

Then, when we don't live up to our potential, we get to be right about how much is really wrong with us. We can return to all the things we do in order to NOT DO what we're really meant to do in life. We have the perfect excuse to maintain the status quo. Back to life as usual. Somewhat satisfying.

Inevitably the time comes when we realize we're not

living our life to the fullest. We're still carrying the proverbial baggage. The old story, the long story we've been dragging around has gotten annoyingly heavy. For me that realization signaled the time had come to take an overview of my life, then honestly and lovingly determine which aspects of my professional, emotional, relational, and spiritual lives were working and which weren't. As you make your overview and go through your list you'll likely notice a connection between the decisions you made early in life about yourself and the early perspectives which still impact your life now.

Perfect memory recall isn't necessary when you start considering the decisions you made about yourself when you were young. But as you move deeper into this practice you'll probably get a sense of the circumstances of your formative stories. Given the nature of the events in your life at that time, you probably made some brilliant decisions based on your need to survive and feel safe. The choices you made in childhood during critical times were beneficial for you then, but hanging on to them as your guiding lights in adulthood is probably neither brilliant nor helpful. Particularly as most of those decisions were made around the assumptions that something must be wrong with you, decisions made at a time when you were scared and uncertain about who you really were.

However, as I said, life demands that we plough on. I can tell you from my experiences that however tempting it might be to hold fast to decisions that served you at an earlier time, you don't have to live the rest of your life with your early interpretations. The point being, the decisions you made that were right for you at a young age have very likely become limiting habits that you've never questioned.

I began to notice that beneath my clients' complaints and judgments there was actually something quite satisfying for them. Rachel came to see me with unexplainable, uncontrollable outbursts of anger toward her husband, coworkers, and sometimes even toward the kids in her first grade classroom. She finally opened up and shared that she and her sister were verbally abused by their father. Nothing she did was good enough in her father's eyes. She was even punished for things she didn't do. I felt her defiance and in fact she had plenty of evidence to back up her interpretation of her father. But as her story gained momentum, it was clear to me she was attached to how she was treated and didn't want to let go of making her father wrong.

As the full story was revealed, she began to release her repressed rage and resentment for how she had been treated. She wrote letters, read them aloud in her sessions, and then burned the letters. She became intentional about letting go of her anger and resentment. Minus all of her judgment and criticism of her father, she came to a greater understanding of what had actually happened and finally understood that her father was just being who he was and he just did what he did. For the first time she remembered all that he had taught her and that she'd used his guidance in her life almost every day. He taught her to build things from the ground up, such as do repairs on her own car. He also informed her about the safest and best use of many tools he had given her and imparted a profound love of nature and the outdoors. By letting go of all that she was so certain was wrong with him, her love for him began to resurface. And she also stopped blaming her husband, coworkers and kids for everything else she was so angry about and started having more fun. This was an unexpected and surprising result for Rachel, who had needed to be right about what was wrong with her father.

I write about this method being a practice. I use it for myself daily, and I know it's not easy. I was in the grocery store recently. I quickly noticed my judgments when I saw the woman in front of me buying a dozen donuts, a gallon of chocolate ice cream, Oreos, and two giant bottles of Coke. When I compared my healthy choices to her junk, I noticed how satisfying it was to feel smug and righteous. I observed my response and took a deep breath. I did so just in time to overhear her tell the checker that she was taking treats to firefighters who had saved her beloved pets from perishing in a house fire.

Yes, after the not so gentle reminder, I took another deep breath and felt relieved to let go of my righteous judgment. I left the store more committed than ever to be more vigilant in my practice, the practice of letting go of judgment, blame and criticism. Way more satisfying.

# Suggested Personal Practices

- What benefits do you get from holding onto judgments and criticisms? If you can be honest about this you have a better chance of letting these 'benefits' go and getting on with what you want to accomplish.

- Think of a time when you misjudged another person or situation. How did you feel?

# 4

*Words, so innocent and powerless as they are as standing in a dictionary, how potent right and wrong become in the hands of one who makes the interpretation.*

~Nathaniel Hawthorne

The many possibilities of a new interpretation will likely call forth questions. Every new interpretation does. I consider questioning a good thing. Those of us already committed to allowing circumstances and events to stand on their own, still wonder how this perspective can work. Particularly when we're designed to live under the rigidity of right or wrong interpretations, leaving us to instantly judge and criticize what we don't immediately understand.

The above deliberation is one of the reasons it took me so long to write this book. And why I continue testing the limits of this reinterpretation every time I encounter a new opportunity.

I know it's difficult to accept the concept that there is nothing wrong when the actions of some people are senseless, brutal and disturbing. I'm in no way minimizing or justifying these acts. It is only human to have painful emotional reactions to the terrible things that some people do, that can include endangering even the people you love. This is not about giving up your core values or your emotional responses when bad things happen. You aren't able to control those reactions anyway. But when you shed some of the blame and judgment about what happened or what someone did, you are better able to move on to your own personal healing in less time, with less effort, and with less struggle.

I find comfort in the words of MacArthur Award

winning author Octavia Butler. Hopefully, when you face senseless and painful circumstances you will also appreciate her wisdom. Butler says there are consequences for the choices people make but to let someone else enforce those consequences. "I don't write about good and evil or right and wrong with this enormous dichotomy," she says. "I write about the kinds of things people do."

I keep reminding myself that I'm writing about a different interpretation that can take us out of judgment, criticism and blame of ourselves and others. Imagine the savings of mental, physical, emotional and spiritual energy you'll experience when there's no longer a right or wrong to defend. Growth is unpredictable. Certainly you will still slip into judgment over and over again. But now you'll take the opportunity to notice it, let it go, and move forward to something you want to accomplish. A way more powerful way for you to be in your world.

During our Sedona Film Festival a few years ago I met one of the film directors who over three consecutive years had documentaries accepted into the festival. When I told him the name of this book, he responded, "Oh, really? I can tell you right now eight things that are wrong with me."

I said, "Name one."

He proudly and quickly responded, "I have Oppositional Defiant Disorder!"

I said, "What's wrong with that?"

He said, "I would openly defy my parents and teachers."

"What's wrong with that?"

"I refused to comply with the rules at school and wouldn't do what I was asked to do at home. I lost my temper often and argued a lot with adults and had very few friends."

"What's wrong with that?" I asked.

And after many more interactions similar to the above, he said: "Well, I actually liked being alone and became very creative. I made up stories and started writing film scripts in my head very early on. Come to think of it, having Oppositional Defiant Disorder led me become the successful director I am."

Not a right or a wrong diagnosis, just accepting *it is what it is*. Much like the old man in the parable you read about in the prologue.

The next morning the director found me and reported he had slept through the night for the first time in years. He felt much better about himself having removed all the criticism and self-incrimination and said he was going to relook at the seven other things he had been so certain were wrong with him.

Elizabeth came to see me because she was stuck in a dead-end job that provided her with the security she needed, but not the opportunity to use her extraordinary creativity. Given she had been at this company for eleven years, the thought of leaving her job and giving notice to her employer left her paralyzed with fear. After several sessions she agreed, reluctantly, to finally give notice.

She came to her next session, but said she had almost cancelled the appointment. She could hardly speak she felt so disappointed in herself for lacking the courage to give notice on her job. I listened patiently and then said, "Elizabeth, what if you just didn't give notice? Is it possible for you to take away the judgment, criticism, and beating yourself up? Can you just say, I didn't give notice?"

It was hard for her to give up her view of herself and she was terrified to stand in the place of 'I didn't give notice.' Her assignment for the week was to say: I didn't give notice, but without all of the additional story she had been creating.

The following week she arrived for her appointment with a big smile on her face. (Usually a pretty good sign.) She had quit her job that week. How did she do it? She placed sticky notes everywhere with the words: I didn't give notice. With nothing else added to those four words, she placed notes in the bathroom mirror, on the fridge, on her iPad, on the dashboard, in a drawer in her office. After a week she walked into her boss's office and gave notice! She felt very accomplished and free and is now happier than she has been for years.

My friend Adam purchased an expensive new flute. He's an accomplished flute player but his intention was to start playing jazz, so he began practicing in that mode to help fulfill a lifelong dream of being in the local band. He soon realized that he would need considerable instruction. After a few challenging and difficult lessons, he lost the momentum. He became overly critical of his ability and found many excuses, such as practicing took too much time, he was too tired at night, and possibly did not have the talent to learn the level of skill required to jam with the locals. He stopped playing, but he didn't stop making himself wrong, and was even remorseful about the money he spent on the new flute. This went on for weeks with more complaining, and still no action toward his goal.

After listening a little longer, I told Adam not to go near his flute for at least a week. I added that when he started feeling judgmental and critical, to simply say: I am not playing my flute right now. PERIOD. I recommended that he say that a couple of times a day without adding anything else. He called me three days later to tell me he was practicing his new flute, had signed up again for lessons, and had made contact with a local band that now wanted to give him an audition. The break from his self-incriminations gave him the freedom to finally pick up his flute and play.

I recently had a client, who after smoking a pack of cigarettes a day for fifteen years, wanted to quit. She had tried everything including hypnotherapy, the patch, nicotine gum, quitting cold turkey, but nothing had been successful. She had spent considerable money on one hypnotherapy session that promised she could quit in an hour. As soon as she got home she lit up!

She came to her appointment angry and disappointed with herself, judgmental about being weak and unable to control the nasty habit. She was now terrified that she might have lung cancer.

I said, "Here's your assignment. Go home this week and just smoke your cigarettes. Take away all the criticism of yourself, all your judgment about your nasty habit, all of your story about what's wrong with you, and just smoke your cigarettes. Each cigarette you smoke, just smoke it. For a week, when the judgments come up, let them go and just smoke."

She followed my advice for six days and quit smoking for the first time in fifteen years. She was finally able to let go of making herself wrong, and instead, start making healthier choices for herself. She also worked up the courage to get a chest x-ray which was, by the way, clear.

I could fill these pages with stories about the success of this practice but I am more interested in yours. Write and tell me how this practice is beginning to work for you.

# Suggested Personal Practices

- Take one thing a day and notice where you have made yourself wrong; e.g. how you look, how you feel, or if you are working hard enough. Turn that criticism around to be *it is what it is*.

- Think about times when you stopped judging yourself, then notice the satisfaction you felt with what you have accomplished.

- Take time each day to be without judgement and criticism of yourself and others.

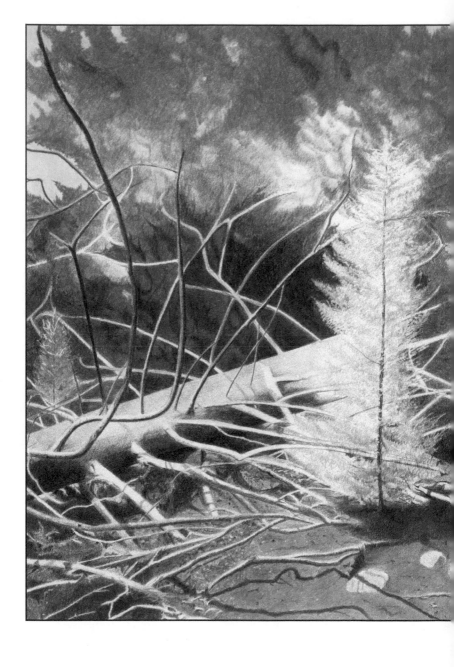

# 5

*Doubt comes in the window when inquiry is denied at the door.* ~Benjamin Jovett

What if there really is something wrong with you? A very personal test of this method occurred in the middle of my writing this book. I had to stop writing and question my own question. Because, yes, I faced a health crisis. I began to doubt if what I was writing about could hold up under the challenging circumstances of life or death. In all honesty, while facing the reality of my heart condition could I even consider asking if there was nothing wrong with me? I had been diagnosed with Congenital Mitral

Valve Prolapse and the valve needed to be replaced. There was clearly urgency required to take the next important steps to fix it. Although it is a condition one can live with for a long time, I realized I HAD lived with the condition for a long time with relatively few symptoms to warn me.

I had been functioning with only forty percent of the blood flow I needed, for how long I'll never know. Each time my heart beat, blood rushed the wrong direction into my left ventricle, enlarging that part of my heart to a dangerous level. It was as if my heart was a rubber band being stretched to maximum and I was in danger of cardiac arrest.

Now what? No more what IF something was wrong with me, when in fact there WAS something wrong with me. Very wrong. Critically wrong. All writing stopped and was replaced by frantic research to find the right surgeon to do a very complicated surgery with huge risks, with potentially serious consequences. The valve had calcified and very few surgeons in my area were willing to take the risk. I was trying to find answers to so many questions, such as who would be willing to take the chance and perform the delicate surgery. And was I willing to take the chance all the while knowing that I had no choice? So now on top of everything else, I had become a liability risk. I was terrified.

I questioned whether any aspect of this practice could apply to having a heart condition that required I undergo a surgery that could either save or end my life. I stopped thinking. I stopped writing. I stopped drawing. I couldn't do much of anything, including taking the next needed steps. Drama began to take over my life. Then after a period of feeling sorry for myself and being terrified, I got it! Once I moved past the hysteria the fact of the matter was simple. I needed a valve replaced and I wasn't writing or drawing. PERIOD. That was all there was.

My brother connected me with the best cardiothoracic surgeon in Houston who had done hundreds of these surgeries with identical complications. Once the valve was replaced, I had more energy than I had before. I used my recovery time to start writing again. I don't mean to minimize the stress that led up to the successful outcome, but when I finally got that I could use the method that I had been writing about and allow these circumstances to exist without interpretation, the stress began to fade into action.

As we get older, the body will present us with challenges that can take us in any number of directions. Fortunately this practice can provide the alternate option that there is nothing wrong, only what IS. This perspective leaves us able to remain in action and find solutions versus being in fear and staying paralyzed.

If you are beginning to accept this concept, you will begin asking about all that seems so wrong and broken with other people and the ongoing terrible occurrences we face every day. It's very difficult to think there is nothing wrong with mass murder or other tragic events. But remember this is a personal inquiry into what if there is nothing wrong with you. When you take the right and wrong filter off of your own judgments and criticisms, you can use this practice to provide a new interpretation to see everything in a new way.

So clearly the message of this book does not imply that bad things don't happen. It is also not about taking away the emotional content of all that we feel and experience, then replacing our thoughts and feelings with magical thinking that claims nothing can harm or bother us. The feelings that follow these terrible events are not to be minimized. Your disappointment, sadness, profound grieving for a deeply felt loss must be expressed and released, and you should do so for as long as it takes. Feelings can't be ignored, as if you could ignore them anyway. But when you can accept that you feel the way you feel, *it is the way that it is*, you can move the feelings through with much more ease and begin to heal the pain.

Your life will consistently, repeatedly and relentlessly bring challenges to confront you, but this practice can provide a contextual shift in how you interpret what does happen, offering an alternative of believing that you, events that happen, illness, even tragedy, are really just what they are. PERIOD.

## Suggested Personal Practices

- Turn one physical challenge you are having into *it is the way it is*. Next, try doing the same with all your physical challenges.

- Can you now accept with less anxiety those things about which you can do nothing? This does NOT mean you have to like it, by the way!

# 6

*To forgive is to set a prisoner free and
discover that the prisoner was you.*
~Louis B. Smedes

If you have been reading this book straight through,
it's now time to put the book down. Take a break.
This has not necessarily been easy reading. You will
need to give yourself a certain amount of permission
at this point to go back over some of your personal
thoughts, and see if there is more you want to say
about your own story; perhaps there is somebody you
are still judging and blaming; or you feel the need to
release emotions that you have held onto for a long

time. Or simply, you want to tell others about how painful it has been to be you, and have them tell you how courageous you've been to have held it together for so long. Yes, I get it. Been there.

And here's where it gets a little more difficult. The next step is to move toward forgiving yourself for the things you have felt, thought, or have done to yourself, and to forgive others for what they have done to you. I think the reason we resist and avoid forgiving is that we think it means condoning or excusing the harm that has been done to us. Or that the offender has gotten away with something, especially if there wasn't any acknowledgment or apology. In that case, consider the benefit that's in it for you to release energy trapped in the form of past resentments. This energy can be returned to you for better use by simply allowing the circumstances to be what they are and events to stand alone without judgement.

When holding a grudge or resentment toward another person you're usually certain that you have a right to feel that way, and of course, the offender is wrong. How, you wonder, do you let go of the anger and resentment? And how do you let go of being right about something you so fervently believe to be true? As author Anne Lamott has described in perfectly vivid language: "Not forgiving is like drinking rat poison then waiting for the rat to die."

Simply put, it's a choice to be willing to let go of being right, thereby freeing yourself from the control that person has or has had over you. It's essential to remember that this practice is about you and your perspective. It has nothing to do with the other person. But unfortunately for you, in ways that you may not be aware of, that person still has a tight grip on how you interact with every subsequent relationship and every new experience you have. The same applies to actions you haven't forgiven yourself for, when in truth, you simply did what you did. PERIOD. Nothing else added.

Forgiving yourself can set you free from your past

and enable you to fulfill your potential, open up new creative channels, enhance your love of self, and can possibly increase your ability to solve problems. I've looked at the long list of ways I have made myself wrong and at the many things I've yet to forgive myself for, and I've also considered the benefits of remaining with the same long held perspectives. When I weighed the consequences compared to what I wanted to accomplish, the list was very unbalanced.

I think of forgiveness as an ongoing process of being willing to experience fully what you are feeling, then allowing it to remain exactly as it is. I recommend to my clients that each time a difficult memory of anger and resentment comes up about themselves or others, they should try choosing to stay in the practice of *it is what it is* and not surround it with energy depleting drama.

Enter this practice slowly and respectfully. Because just like any new subject that you set out to learn, it will take practice.

My earliest experience of trying to practice forgiveness

was with the most difficult person in my life: my father. Frankly, I wasn't very successful. I only wish I'd had the resources then that I have now. I try to imagine what my relationship would have been with him if I could have allowed him to be just who he was and not have to live up to some hopeful fantasy about what I thought a father should be. At least my client Rachel received the benefit of the good parts of her relationship with her father.

My father has been gone for years, and I am now clear that I had no space for him in my life and had little if any compassion for what he must have been going through with his illness. Perhaps the best thing I can do now is quit making myself wrong and support others going through similar issues. I did the best I could, and he did the best he could do with the hand he was dealt. I continue to thank him for providing me with material to work on myself. Yes, it continues. But through time and practice I've finally forgiven my father and now feel compassion for his unfortunate circumstances. After all, he was being exactly who he was.

We are often blind to observing ourselves from the inside out. I do know that one of the ways to begin this practice is to accept that you are the way you are and you did what you did. PERIOD. It is a powerful practice to support you in clearing the past and in forgiving yourself. We are doomed to repeat the past when the cycle of unresolved issues keeps showing up in our current life and we haven't learned new ways of interacting with those issues.

In your ongoing practice of forgiving yourself, you will find that unacknowledged and untapped resources will emerge and you will discover that you are more capable and stronger than you ever imagined. Forgiveness takes time. Don't be hard on yourself. Those old thoughts and beliefs about yourself have defined you and even held you together in many ways.

# Suggested Personal Practices

- Make a list of things you have not forgiven yourself for.

- Make another list of those people you have not forgiven.

- Write a letter (that you don't send!) expressing your anger or resentment, love or appreciation.... Do this with the intention of being finished with that part of your story.

# 7

*The last of the human freedoms - to choose one's attitude in any given set of circumstances, to choose one's own way.*

*~Viktor Frankl*

Life is a matter of making choices, isn't it? When we begin to notice all the ways we have designed our lives around what is wrong, the observer of that designer is born. We begin to see from a place of observation what we have been thinking, deciding, judging, plotting, and figuring out. It can be very interesting and possibly a little upsetting to discover that our judgments about ourselves and the choices we made have been based on the person we have often judged as being in the wrong. The concept of choice begins to show up when we move from judging ourselves to being aware of our behavior.

Through the eyes of the observer you start seeing what you are doing over and over, and that ability gives you the option to choose a different way of being or doing. You can even choose to keep doing the same things as you do now, but you will be aware that you have choices that maybe weren't available before. You are now noticing things that haven't worked, and you can stop being so shocked that life keeps giving you the same old crap.

So finally, if you now believe there is nothing wrong with you, your choices will have expanded beyond whatever you thought was possible. You can select any, all, or none of the new options, but at the least you now have choices. No longer do you need all the constraints that you have systematically and methodically put upon yourself.

My first marriage at twenty-two was somewhat based on the belief that it was time to get married. After all I had no plans after graduation from college and maybe I wouldn't get asked again. And honestly, Richard, my first husband, was so unlike my father I couldn't resist. I am clear, given the eventual outcome of the marriage, that neither of us chose from a conscious place.

Richard is now happily married to Roger and they have been together for close to thirty years. Eric and I are in a loving, communicative relationship and married for forty-one years. Richard and I chose our next relationships with a lot more information than we had when we chose each other. The good news is we have two wonderful sons with lovely wives, and we all share two beautiful grandchildren.

When we make important decisions based on a past where we decided that so much was wrong with us, the outcome rarely works.

I hadn't thought of this until I started writing but I think that the clearest choice I ever made for myself was when I was twelve. Our family was on a driving trip from Kentucky up through Ohio that ended on the East Coast. We were in Provincetown on the tip of Cape Cod where I observed several plein air artists at work. When I stopped to watch an artist painting the scene in front of him, I said, with absolute certainty at that moment: "I can do that!"

I made a choice right there and have been painting and drawing since then. And come to think of that moment, I have no doubt this decision came more from my gut than from any wisdom about  choice. This photograph captures that moment when there was nothing wrong with me and it just was the way it was, minus any of my old story. I have kept that old photo in my studio to remind me of that early moment of clarity.

As I continue clearing self-recriminations from the past, I'm beginning to remember more experiences of making choices from uninformed perspectives. There was a time when I was a kid that looking in the mirror was a painful experience filled with so much judgment and criticism I could barely see who was there. I thought I was an odd looking child. Imagine a girl with freckles, funny teeth, big eyes, and straight, fine hair. Of course, as you might guess, my mother desperately wanted a little girl with curls.

I recently stood in front of my mirror for ten minutes and looked at the person looking back at me as if she were someone else. I asked myself: "If I saw that woman coming toward me, would I want to be her friend?"

I kept staring at her, separating who I was from who was coming toward me. The answer finally came loud and clear: "YES, I like her, and I want to be her friend." I loved myself at that moment and can now choose that feeling when I want to. And finally I do so more often than not.

I recently met a woman on a plane who had lost her husband of twenty-five years. When I told her about the premise of my book, she said she liked the concept and believed in it. She continued by sharing her experience following the death of her husband. "When my husband died after a four-month illness, I had an interesting experience grieving his loss. Other people in my life thought my grieving process should look a different way, that it should be longer, that I shouldn't be feeling okay quite yet and shouldn't be in another relationship so fast. But my husband and I had an opportunity to say all the things we wanted to say and we felt so grateful for the time we had together. I chose to grieve exactly how I wanted to, not how others thought it should look. I feel complete and that there is nothing wrong with me."

# Suggested Personal Practices

- Make some new life choices without judging or criticizing yourself.

- Take some time to be with yourself in your mirror. Consider if you if you would like to be a friend with the person whose image you see. What are your thoughts as you look into the mirror? I had to look away a couple of times before coming back. Hang in there. You are worth it.

- Return to the list you made of things you believe are wrong with you and see if you can cross out a few.

# 8

*It is through accomplishment that we make our contribution and contribution is life's greatest reward.*

~John Portman, Architect

CONGRATULATIONS! You've done most of the hard work and now you get to the part that's fun, satisfying, with long lasting benefits! I appreciate your courage in taking this journey with me. I invite you to consider the reward of making a contribution that will provide benefits long after you're gone.

If you've been vigilant with your practice, it's likely

you are noticing results. This practice is ongoing, because as we know, life provides us with never-ending opportunities to witness ourselves making judgments. Although I've done my best to integrate this practice, I continue to be surprised how frequently my judgments take over. You may not be able to stop your mind from judging, but you do have the ability now to be the observer of your judgments and move on to some other way of thinking that will likely be more productive.

I think often about my two grandchildren and how I can help release them from the burden of defining themselves from a position of right or wrong. I believe if we teach the young early on about creating their own powerful story they will enter their lives with more confidence, less fear, more imagination, and more willingness to learn and try new things. Fortunately it's never too late to lessen their burden. By modeling this practice we have an opportunity to help shape the future of the children and thereby the future of our society. Yes, we can guide and even discipline the little ones without rewards and punishments of being either right or wrong, and continue to instill core values at the same time. In fact, because a child's innate sense of fairness is still intact, I believe the young are able to more fully understand the real meaning of *it is what it is*.

For the most part, I want to believe that we as a culture are in agreement that the individual's contribution to the whole of society is the real benefit of a life well lived, as well as the key to a personally fulfilling life. Now that I'm in my seventies, I'm clear that I want to leave something that will continue after I'm gone. Imagine a world long after any of us are here, where hearts are opened wide with acceptance and inclusion, where judgment melts into *it is what it is*, and a time when relationships have broken through the barriers of hate and mistrust.

Although this book starts with you (as if there were any other place to start) the possibilities are limitless in every direction you can see. I know I have made a difference in the way many people now look at themselves. I know they are happier because of our encounter, be it in their personal or professional life. I know I've made a difference and I'm sure you know that you too have impacted the lives of others.

The lasting value in all of this is that as we change, so do others we relate to, and therefore so does the world. The ripple effect of a practice of acceptance, respect, and non-judgment is never-ending.

I am not so naive to think that this is a panacea for all problems. Rather, this a powerful question to keep in front of your mind, a ready place to go when you fall into that old place of self-doubt.

Hey, what if there really IS nothing wrong with you? Use this question as a practice that you ask yourself when you wake up. By doing so, it is likely you will have more choices that will lead to a life full of love and contribution.

Remember, like anything you do that's new, practice is the ongoing key. I promise it will be challenging from time to time, but completely worth it in the long haul.

# *Suggested Personal Practices*

- Keep track of the benefits that show up in your life when you adopt the practice of *what if there is nothing wrong with you.*

- As a launch for you to create your own empowering and liberating manifesto below are a few of my entries as examples:

  *I have finally learned to understand who I am and accept who I am not. That has set me free.*

  *I am a loyal friend.*

  *I am not a judgmental person but when it comes up, I am willing to let it go.*

  *I appreciate all that is beautiful in my world.*

  *I am a careful listener.*

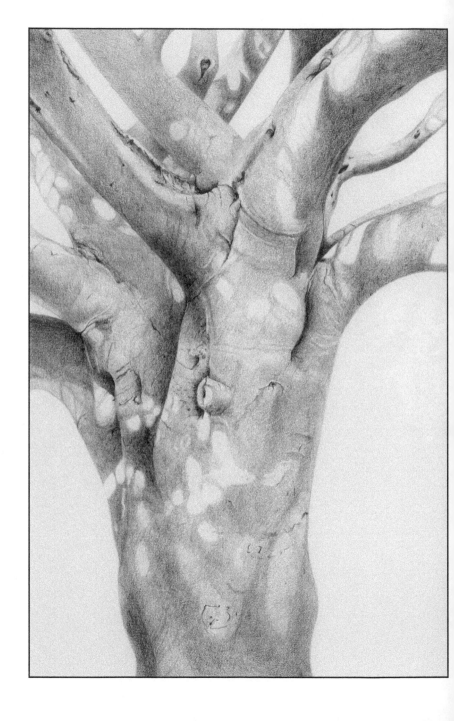

# Epilogue

*"When you go out into the woods and you look at trees, you see all these different trees. And some of them are bent, and some of them are straight ... And you look at the tree and you allow it. ... You sort of understand that it didn't get enough light, and so it turned that way. And you don't get all emotional about it. You just allow it. You appreciate the tree. The minute you get near humans, you lose all that. And you are constantly saying 'You're too this, or I'm too this.' That judging mind comes in. And so I practice turning people into trees. Which means appreciating them just the way they are."* - Ram Dass

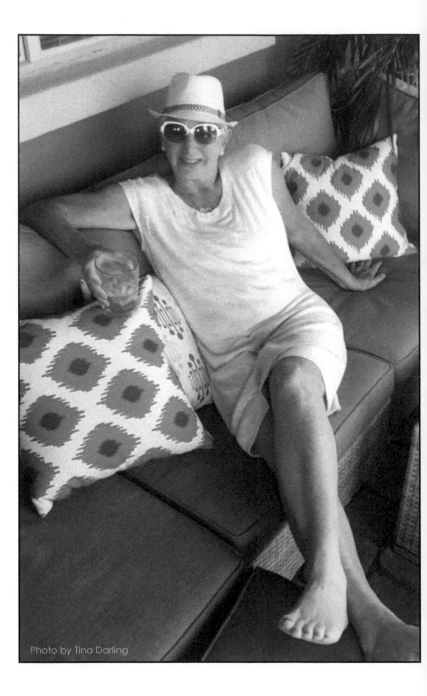

# Acknowledgements

So many of you have been a part of the team that have supported the ongoing work of this project from clients and their generous stories, friends who have offered to read and give input, and family who have kept me in my own practice of What if there is nothing wrong with you! You know who you are. Ethan, Rebecca, Dorian, and Julie you are also deeply loved and appreciated and you asked good questions along the way. Miles and Chloe, this is actually all for you. You will both be the creators of a whole new world of possibilities.

Special thank you to the original creative women's circle who heard about it first and validated the idea and were also powerful devil's advocates. Jennifer Epperson, Debra Beck, Danette Wolpert, and Jane Perini who gave me the perfect prologue parable. Thank you, Kathleen Schafer, for our original writing together which took us both in different powerful directions using this concept.

And so much love for Melissa Andrea and Judy Ellickson who were my encouraging drawing buddies every week for fifteen years. So much creativity was generated in that studio.

Special thanks to Linda Horn, Alan Davidson, Dawn Shattuck and Jim Heynen for their valuable feedback early on. And to Rhea Philo and Margaret Joy Weaver who have relentlessly encouraged me along the way to keep moving out of my comfort zone. Deep gratitude to my dearest friend, Cindy Paine, who has listened carefully, supported me through all the bumps and grinds of growing, and has loved me unconditionally.

Much appreciation to my incredibly competent tech team Myss Miranda, Gary Glenn and Tim Fox who always made me, this book and my art work shine throughout.

Thank you to my brother, Richard Munich, M.D., whose input on some of our history was invaluable and his feedback and support on this idea, even through his skepticism, was encouraging and very much appreciated.

And to Sunday Larson ... where do I begin? Her

creativity and lightening bolt ideas as my writing coach and editor added a whole new dimension to this project and I am deeply grateful for her patience, partnership, and unwillingness to buy into anything being wrong with me. Thank you from my heart.

And finally, my greatest debt is to my best buddy, pal, and husband, Eric Henkels. His suggestions and additions were always right on but more importantly, his willingness to read and reread and hold my hand to steer me on track when I wasn't sure what to do next. I love you.

# Forthcoming Titles
## by Susan M. Henkels, MSW

*What if There's Nothing Wrong With Lucy*, an inspiring book for children and their parents.

*What if There's Nothing Wrong With Your Kid*, a reminder for parents to stop and reconsider when judging and criticizing their children.

*Pause Under the Trees*: A book of reflections for when your mind needs a rest.

Coming Soon! Facebook and forum opportunities for you to participate in the conversation examining the premise of the book *What if There is Nothing Wrong With You?* by Susan M. Henkels, MSW. After all, our stories are our best teachers, and as was said by Paul Wellstone: "We all do better when we all do better."

Ms. Henkels is available to work with you individually, as a couple, as a family, or within your organization to more effectively use the distinctions found in her book *What If There is Nothing Wrong With You.*

Retreat Dates, Speaking Engagements, Book Reviews, Reader Comments, and Good News is updated regularly on her website: www. susanmunichhenkels.com.

A portion of the poceeds from this book will be donated to One Tree Planted, a 501(C 3), non profit organization focused on planting trees around the world. One dollar, one tree.

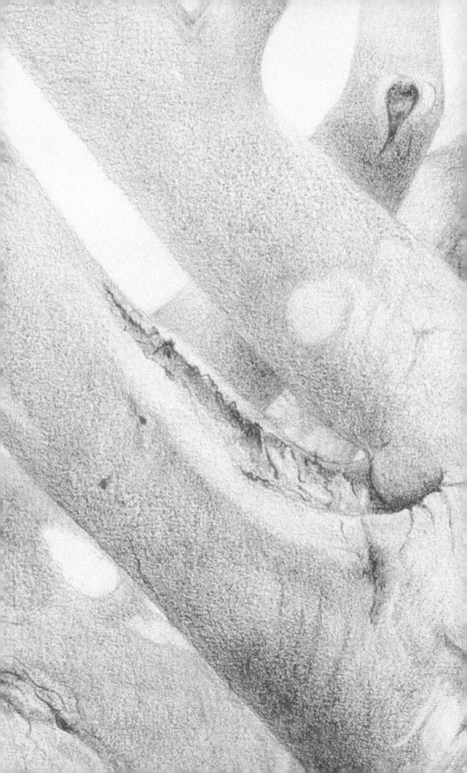

*Excerpts From*

# Pauses

— a Book of Reflections —

*by Susan M. Henkels, MSW*

*We spend an enormous amount of energy making up our minds about other people. Not a day goes by without somebody doing or saying something that evokes in us the need to form an opinion about him or her. We hear a lot, see a lot, and know a lot. The feeling that we have to sort it all out in our minds and make judgments about it can be quite oppressive. The desert fathers said that judging others is a heavy burden while being judged by others is a light one. When we can let go of our need to edge others, we will experience an immense inner freedom.*

~ Henri Nouwen

*Buddha describes the goal of the path as the "ending of the effluents." As human beings we're subject to a variety of experiences: sights, sounds, smells, tastes, bodily sensations, mental impressions (thoughts, emotions). None of these experiences- whether pleasant or unpleasant - is a problem; our "problems" manifest in the effluents, the ways we add on to experience, the ways we oppose and pursue experience, the ways we corrupt experience, the ways we take what is and turn it into something else.*

~ The Nava Sutta

*Don't spend your life believing a story about yourself that you didn't write that's been fed to you - that simply you've accepted, embedded, and added to. Let the story go and there beneath is the real you ...  and your unique gifts, heart and path that await you.*

~Rasheed Ogunlaru

*I'm always amazed by how readily people judge the right and wrong of things they know only from the outside. Honestly, it kind of pisses me off.*
~David Clawson - My Fairy Godmother is a drag queen

*Judging is preventing us from understanding a new truth. Free yourself from the rules of old judgments and create the space for new understanding.*
~Steve Mariboldi

*The hardest times in your life to go through are when you are transitioning from one version of yourself to another.*
~Sarah Addison Allen

*Excellence is never an accident. It is always the result of high intention, sincere effort, and intelligent execution; it represents the wise choice of many alternatives - choice, not chance, determines your destiny.*

~ Aristotle

*We have a choice. We can spend our whole life suffering because we can't relax with how things really are, or we can relax and embrace the open-mindedness of the human situation, which is fresh, unfixated, unbiased.*

~ Perna Chodron

*In Zen there is an old saying: The obstacle is the path. Know that a whole and happy life is not free of obstacles. Quite the contrary, a whole and happy life is riddled with obstacles - they simply become the very stepping stones that help lift us to a new perspective. It is not what happens to us in this life that shapes us, it is how we choose to respond to what happens to us.*

~ Dennis Merritt Jones

*Be the one who nurtures and builds. Be the one who has an understanding and a forgiving heart who looks for the best in people. Leave people better than you found them.*

~ Marvin Ashton

*Forgiveness is not something you do for someone else; it's something you do for yourself. To forgive is not to condone; it is to refuse to continue feeling bad about an injury.*

~ Jim Beaver

*Forgiveness is not a one off decision; it is a journey and a process that takes time, determination, and persistence. Forgiveness is not forgetting; it is simply denying your pain the right to control your life.*

~ Corallie Buchanan

*Life is too short to wake up in the morning with regrets. So, love the people who treat you right, forgive the ones who don't, and believe that everything happens for a reason. If you get the chance, take it. If it changes your life, let it. Nobody said it would be easy, they just promised it would be worth it.*

~ Dr. Seuss

*The healer you have been looking for is your own courage to know and love yourself completely.*

~ Yung Pueblo

*No one is harder on me than me. So take your judgment and shove it up your ass.*

~ Author Unknown

*Let us be grateful to the mirror for revealing to us our appearance only.*
~ Samuel Butler

*Ah, nothing is too late, till the tired heart shall cease to palpitate.*

~ Henry Wadsworth Longfellow

*My mother's menu existed of two choices:*

*Take it or leave it.*

~ Buddy Hackett

*Your time is limited, so don't waste it living someone else's life. Don't be trapped by dogma - which is living with the results of other people's thinking. Don't let the noise of others' opinions drown out your own inner voice. And most important, have the courage to follow your heart and intuition.*

~ Steve Jobs

## THE ROAD NOT TAKEN

*Two roads diverged in a yellow wood,*
*And sorry I could not travel both*
*And be one traveler, long I stood*
*And looked down one as far as I could*
*To where it bent in the undergrowth;*

*Then took the other, as just as fair,*
*And having perhaps the better claim,*
*Because it was grassy and wanted wear;*
*Though as for that, the passing there*
*Had worn them really about the same,*

*And both that morning equally lay*
*In leaves no step had trodden black.*
*Oh, I kept the first for another day!*
*Yet knowing how way leads on to way,*
*I doubted if I should ever come back.*

*I shall be telling this with a sign*
*Somewhere ages and ages hence:*
*Two roads diverged in a wood, and I –*
*I took the one less traveled by,*
*And that has made all the difference.*

*~ Robert Frost*

# Notes

# Notes

# Notes

# Notes

# Suggested Reading

OUTLIVING THE SELF, *by John Kotre*

A MORE BEAUTIFUL
QUESTION, *by Warren Berger*

CHANGE YOUR QUESTION, CHANGE
YOUR LIFE, *by Marilee Adams*

LOVING WHAT IS, *by Byron Katie*

BECOMING WHAT YOU ARE, *by Alan Watts*

THE PARENT'S TAO TE CHING
*Ancient Advice for Modern Parents, by William Martin*

I AND THOU, *by Martin Buber*

SELF OBSERVATION: THE AWAKENING
OF CONSCIENCE, *by Red Hawk*

CLEAR CONNECT CREATE, *by Cindy Paine*

*You may find yourself wanting to read and re-read <u>this</u> book.*
*What if there's nothing wrong with <u>that</u>?*